GROOMED TO GROOM

WRITTEN BY

EDNA RUTH HOOKER HALL, D. TH.

ISBN 979-8-88955-522-3

GROOMED TO GROOM

TABLE OF CONTENTS

PRELUDE

Blessed assurance, Jesus is mine. Oh, what a foretaste of glory divine. Heir of salvation, purchase of God. Born of His spirit, washed in His blood.

Perfect submission, all is at rest. I, in my Savior, am happy and blessed. Watching and waiting, looking above. Filled with His goodness, lost in His love.

This is my story; this is my song—praising my Savior all the day long. This is my story; this is my song— Praising my Savior all the day long.

Have you ever wondered why you went through the things that you went through in life, or the things you are going through right now? You are not the only one. All of us have a story. In every one of our stories, there was/is some good and some bad. It is good to know that God knows how to fashion it all so it will work together for our good. I pray that my story will assist you in your journey to completion, as it has propelled me into the place where I trust God above and beyond all else. Be blessed and encouraged as you grow through your grooming process.

ACKNOWLEDGEMENTS

As I sit back and think over my life, I thank God for being true to His word. I conclude like Paul in 2nd Timothy 1:12, "For I know whom I have believed and am persuaded that He is able to keep that which I have committed unto Him against that Day." He has never lost a battle and He never will. He has done all of that and more. I am so grateful also for all the support I received from my family and friends. I thank God for every spiritual mentor that God placed

in my life. So many have gone on to be with the Lord since I started writing this masterpiece, *Groomed to Groom.* Since the publishing of my first book, "Surviving Spiritual Boot Camp," some of my spiritual mentors have transitioned to be with the Lord: Eldress Georgia Lewis, Bishop Ernest O. Edwards, Assistant to the Bishop, Elder Michael

Whitfield, and Eldress Mildred Ross. I'm so grateful for every impartation they placed on my life. They indeed groomed me to be what and who I am today in my walk with Christ.

Still giving me guidance is Bishop Johnnie Ervin Reddick, who has suffered a major stroke since I started pinning this book, as well as Apostle Polly Elliott and Eldress Ora Kornegay (not pictured). They always take time out to talk to me no matter when I call them. Each one of them poured into my life in diverse ways.

In 2009, Bishop Reddick appointed me as one of his Administrative Assistants. As a member of the Northwest B Annual Conference for fifty years, I still count it an honor to be able to serve such a prestigious man of God. I have learned so much from him and I enjoy serving under his leadership.

DEDICATION

I give honor to God for all He has done for me. There have been so many mountains and valleys in my life. Some were easier to overcome than others. If it had not been for the grace of God, I would have never made it. I thank Him for every chance He gave me to get it right, despite my complaining and murmuring. Sometimes I felt like just giving up, but God held me closely and I did not let go.

I am thankful for the prayer warriors God surrounded me with during while going through. I give praise to God for the Chara Ministries Deliverance Center family for trusting in my leadership ability, especially during this pandemic we are experiencing. We have been doing our services, including bible study and prayer meetings, virtually since March 2020, and they have been consistent and faithful. God has truly been faithful, and we have not been lacking in any good thing, just as God promised. None of this has happened without opposition, but God delivered us out of them all. We are still standing.

GROOMED TO GROOM

INTRODUCTION

Grooming: What does it mean to groom? It can have a negative meaning, as well as a positive meaning.

1. Negative grooming is when someone builds a relationship, trust, and an emotional connection with a person so they can manipulate them. Children and young people are major targets. They tend to be groomed to be sexually abused, exploited, or trafficked easier. According to *www.nspcc.org.uk*, "Anybody can be a groomer, no matter their age, gender or race." Sometimes it takes a sharp eye to target them.

2. Positive grooming, according to Wikitionary, is "when someone is preparing a person for a position requiring skilled behavior, especially by providing opportunity for practice and guidance in making the right decisions."

All of us have been groomed by someone: positively, negatively, or both. Sometimes it can be the same person. I invite you to come on this journey with me. I have experienced both types of grooming. The negative almost destroyed me, but God wouldn't let it. He blocked the devourer. The positive built me up in my most holy faith and propelled me into my destiny. Truly it was the Lord's doing. Jeremiah 29:11 (KJV) states, "For I know the thoughts that I think toward you, saith the LORD, thoughts of peace, and not of evil, to give you an expected end."

Where does the grooming begin? It begins at birth. We are all groomed from birth until you leave this earth. We are placed in environments that will groom us emotionally, mentally, physically, spiritually, and financially. We experience grooming positively and negatively in all areas of our lives. We decide which road to take towards our expected end. Fantasia Burrino Taylor sings this song—Necessary—that says, "I am who I am today because God used my mistakes. He worked them for my good, like no one else ever could." I just want to tell you every bit of it—the good, the bad, the ugly, and the sad—was necessary.

Without a doubt, I was groomed to groom. I made many mistakes along the way but through confession, repentance, and turning, I'm still standing. Exercising humility and having a teachable spirit made grooming easier. No, I didn't like some of the methods used in my grooming, but it definitely brought me to a good place. A happy place.

In The pictures are Alice Edwards, Hattie Hooker, James T., Edna, Jessie, Thomas, Robert, Geraldine (Deceased), Addie, and David. I also have ten other siblings not pictured, whom I love dearly also: Velma Bynum, Jackie Wooten, Christy Wooten, Myra Wooten, Wilma Davis (Deceased), Raymond Wooten, Jr., Elvis Wooten (Deceased), Willis Wooten, Eddie Wooten (Deceased), and Kassaun Wooten.

CHAPTER 1

GROOMED TO GROOM

We have all been through the process of being groomed. Whether it was good or bad, we were groomed.

"3 Blessed be God, even the Father of our Lord Jesus Christ, the Father of mercies, and the God of all comfort; 4 Who comforteth us in all our tribulation, that we may be able to comfort them which are in any trouble, by the comfort wherewith we ourselves are comforted of God. 5 For as the sufferings of Christ abound in us, so our consolation also aboundeth by Christ. 6 And whether we be afflicted, it is for your consolation and salvation, which is effectual in the enduring of the same sufferings which we also suffer: or whether we be comforted, it is for your consolation and salvation." - **2nd Corinthians 1:3-6**

Oftentimes we succumb to past traumas and experiences. We get stuck in our feelings and start crying out, 'Lord, why did I have to go through all of that? Or, why do I have to go through all of this?'—

especially as Christians. We forget what the word tells us.

Matthew 5:45 KJV - "That ye may be the children of your Father which is in heaven: for he maketh his sun to rise on the evil and on the good, and sendeth rain on the just and on the unjust."

There is no exception to the rule. We voice other expressions such as woe is me and why me? or, "if it ain't one thing, it's another." At the time of our trials and tribulations, we don't stop to think that God is allowing us to be groomed so that we can be fit for His use.

2nd Timothy 2:21 KJV - "If a man therefore purge himself from these, he shall be a vessel unto honour, sanctified, and meet for the master's use, and prepared unto every good work."

But God is calling for us to accept what He has allowed, with the assurance that He won't put no more on us than we can bear.

1 Corinthians 10:13 KJV - "There hath no temptation taken you but such as is common to man: but God is faithful, who will not suffer you to be tempted above that ye are able; but will with the temptation also make a way to escape, that ye may be able to bear it."

We are fearfully and wonderfully made, and He knows what we can handle. We may not want to, but it's not about us; it's all about the Kingdom. We are groomed to groom. As we already established, groom means to prepare or train (someone) for a particular purpose or activity. We are God's elect. His chosen generation. His peculiar people. His royal priesthood. We've been trained to train by the best trainer that ever lived. His name is Jesus. We have definitely been GROOMED TO GROOM!

We say we are doing like Paul. He said:

Philippians 3:7-17 KJV - "7 But what things were gain to me, those I counted loss for Christ. 8 Yea doubtless, and I count all things but loss for the excellency of the knowledge of Christ Jesus my Lord: for whom I have suffered the loss of all things, and do count them but dung, that I may win Christ, 9 And be found in him, not having mine own righteousness, which is of the law, but that which is through the faith of Christ, the righteousness which is of God by faith: 10 That I may know him, and the power of his resurrection, and the fellowship of his sufferings, being made conformable unto his death; 11 If by any means I might attain unto the resurrection of the dead. 12 Not as though I had already attained, either were already perfect: but I follow after, if that I may apprehend that for which also, I am apprehended of Christ Jesus. 13 Brethren, I count not myself to have apprehended: but this one thing I do, forgetting those things which are behind, and reaching forth unto those things which are before, 14 I press toward the mark for the prize of the high calling of God in Christ Jesus."

Philippians 3:2-6 MSG - "Steer clear of the barking dogs, those religious busybodies, all bark and no bite. All they're interested in is appearances knife-happy circumcisers, I call them. The real believers are the ones the Spirit of God leads to work away at this ministry, filling the air with Christ's praise as we do it. We couldn't carry this off by our own efforts, and we know it—even though we can list what many might think are impressive credentials···"

It means absolutely nothing if it flesh-laced. Maybe your walls are filled with degrees and

accomplishments, and your trophy case overrunning with trophies and what nots. But is your heart filled with His spirit? We are told to be filled with the spirit. Oftentimes Paul was taunted because he did not have credentials of his accomplishments. He said, "5 Not that we are sufficient of ourselves to think anything as of ourselves; but our sufficiency is of God; 6 Who also hath made us able ministers of the New Testament; not of the letter, but of the spirit: for the letter killeth, but the spirit giveth life."
- **2nd Corinthians 3:5-6, KJV.**

Philippians 3:2-21 MSG - Verse 2-6 is a continuation of the aforementioned scripture.

"⋯You know my pedigree: a legitimate birth, circumcised on the eighth day; an Israelite from the elite tribe of Benjamin; a strict and devout adherent to God's law; a fiery defender of the purity of my religion, even to the point of persecuting the church; a meticulous observer of everything set down in God's law Book.

7-9 The very credentials these people are waving around as something special, I'm tearing up and throwing out with the trash—along with everything else I used to take credit for. And why? Because of Christ. Yes, all the things I once thought were so important are gone from my life. Compared to the high privilege of knowing Christ Jesus as my Master, firsthand, everything I once thought I had going for me is insignificant—dog dung. I've dumped it all in the trash so that I could embrace Christ and be embraced by him. I didn't want some petty, inferior brand of righteousness that comes from keeping a list of rules when I could get the robust kind that comes from trusting Christ—God's righteousness.

10-11 I gave up all that inferior stuff so I could know Christ personally, experience his resurrection power, be a partner in his suffering, and go all the way with him to death itself. If there was any way to get in on the resurrection from the dead, I wanted to do it.

12-14 I'm not saying that I have this all together, that I have it made. But I am well on my way, reaching out for Christ, who has so wondrously reached out for me. Friends don't get me wrong: By no means do I count myself an expert in all of this, but I've got my eye on the goal, where God is beckoning us onward—to Jesus. I'm off and running, and I'm not turning back. 15-16 So let's keep focused on that goal, those of us who want everything God has for us. If any of you have something else in mind, something less than total commitment, God will clear your blurred vision—you'll see it yet! Now that we're on the right track, let's stay on it.

17-19 Stick with me, friends. Keep track of those you see running this same course, headed for this same goal. There are many out there taking other paths, choosing other goals, and trying to get you to go along with them. I've warned you of them many times; sadly, I'm having to do it again. All they want is an easy street. They hate Christ's Cross. But easy street is a dead-end street. Those who live there make their bellies their gods; belches are their praise; all they can think of is their appetites.

20-21 But there's far more to life for us. We're citizens of high heaven! We're waiting the arrival of the Savior, the Master, Jesus Christ, who will transform our earthy bodies into glorious bodies like his own. He'll make us beautiful and whole with the same powerful skill by which he is putting everything as it should be, under and around him.

Paul also said in 2nd Corinthians chapter one, verses 3 through seven, "3-5 All praise to the God and Father of our Master, Jesus the Messiah! Father of all mercy! God of all healing counsel! He comes alongside us when we go through hard times, and before you know it, he brings us alongside someone else who is going through hard times so that we can be there for that person just as God was there for us. We have plenty of hard times that come from following the Messiah, but no more so than the good times of his healing comfort—we get a full measure of that, too.

6-7 When we suffer for Jesus, it works out for your healing and salvation. If we are treated well, given a helping hand and encouraging word, that also works to your benefit, spurring you on, face forward, unflinching. Your hard times are also our hard times. When we see that you're just as willing to endure the hard times as to enjoy the good times, we know you're going to make it, no doubt about it."

Look at it as you're being groomed for something greater. A lot of my childhood was hard, but God used it all to groom me. As the song says, "For every mountain you brought me over. For every trial You've seen me through, for every blessing—hallelujah—for this, I give You praise." From the bottom of my heart, I praise Him for always being there for me.

CHAPTER 2

THE GROOMING BEGINS

Groomed for Nurturing: This house (the "shotgun house" as it was called back then) is all covered with weeds, vines, and trees. It is located in

Snow Hill, North Carolina on Arba Road, now referenced as Hull Road. In this house, I learned how to raise a family. My grandmother taught me how to cook, clean the house, make quilts, do laundry, do

hair, and everything else I needed to know to maintain a household. I was second to the oldest of my siblings. We were aged 13 years old down to 4 years old. There were 7 of us; there were only 4 rooms.

The living room and the 3 girls' room were one room. Four boys were in one room, grandparents in one, and then there was the kitchen. My grandmother taught me how to stretch a meal. No one ever left the table hungry. She told me the week before she died, just before they took her to Chapel Hill, N.C., that I was going to have to take care of my sisters and brothers. I didn't know she was telling me she wasn't coming back home. She had ovarian cancer. I nearly lost my mind when they told me she was dead. I wouldn't talk or eat. I was angry. Her death left a big hole in my heart.

My mother lived in Washington, D.C. When my grandmother passed, she moved to N.C. to take care of us, bringing one more baby to the fold. He was only six months old. My mother, at thirty-one years old, was now facing the challenge of raising eight children—ages ranging now from thirteen down to six months.

Now I understood what my grandmother was saying. I would have to help raise my siblings. She groomed me well. It seemed so unfair to me that I always had to stay behind. However, it taught me how to be responsible. Being only twelve years old at the time was not even an issue. She had groomed me. It was now time to implement what she had instilled within me. My mother had to go to work, so that left me there to help with the children. It wasn't easy and I did not like it, but I understand it all now. I was being groomed to groom.

These were the siblings I took care of until the other three came along. I became a tomboy, but I loved every bit of it. I climbed trees, swung on vines, jumped brooks, skated on ice covered fields, and played with all their trucks because they destroyed every doll I ever owned. We had a lot of fun. There was never a dull moment. I learned how to be strong when I didn't even know what I was being strong for. The other three came in 1961, 1963, and 1967, two girls and one boy respectively. I was almost 13. I was groomed to groom, and I am still being groomed.

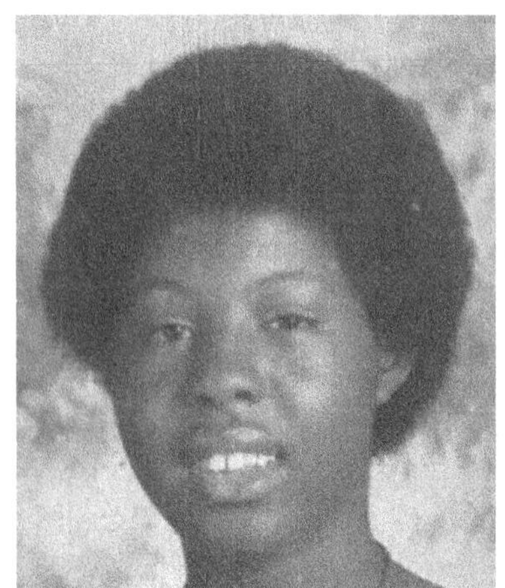

CHAPTER THREE
WORK ETHICS

Picking cotton

Tobacco (planting, suckling, cropping, looping, hanging, etc.)

Picking Cucumbers

School Bus driver #13

Cosmetology

Quilting by hand

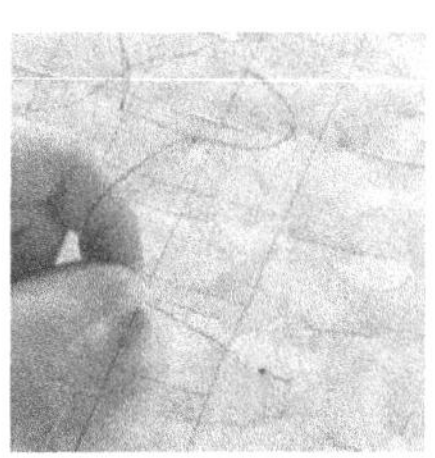

Boiling pots (collards, potatoes, beans, turnip)
Housing, bathroom, heating, laundry

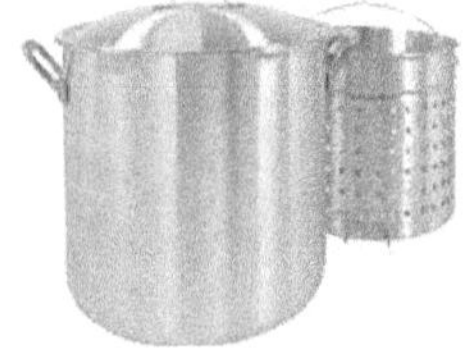

This is how we lived. God is faithful. It groomed me. 3rd grade, 8 years old

Groomed to work. Working was not a stranger to me. The pictures shown above show what I loved to do the best, which was picking cotton, driving my bus, and taking care of my siblings. It also showed what I hated the worse: picking cucumbers. The other job pictured is working in tobacco (looping it, passing it up in the barn to be hung and cured, cropping it, suckling it, taking it out of the barn after it cured, tying it, putting it on the sticks, and loading it on the trucks.

I also plucked corn, picked huckleberries and beans on different farms. After I received my driver's license, I went on to get my bus driver's license. I drove a school bus for three years: Bus 13. I loved it. This ended my cucumber picking. Glory to God!

After I graduated from Greene Central High School in June 1973, I got married in November 1973 to Isaac Hall (1973-2018). My dream was to go to Oral Roberts University and Fayetteville State University, but I started doing factory work. I hemmed pants for four years at Blue Bell in LaGrange, N.C.   For three years, I made transformers at TRW in Kinston, N.C. From June 1973 until September 1980, my heart bled. I was not fulfilling my dreams. Nothing that I wanted to do was happening.

Back in the days, when someone died, they would bring the bodies back to the house for a whole week. When they brought my grandmother to the house, I slept on the stand underneath her casket every night. Every day before my grandmother passed away, I would watch her do my two sisters' hair. As she laid in that casket her hair got uglier and uglier. Every time I looked at it, I wanted to scream. Her grooming paid off.

"Cosmetology" was not in my dreams, but it was a part of God's plan to bring me to my expected end. "For I know the thoughts that I think toward you, saith the Lord, thoughts of peace, and not of evil, to give you an expected end (Jeremiah 29:11, KJV)." Watching my grandma do my sisters' hair taught me how to do hers when she passed away. I didn't like how the funeral home people fixed her hair. When everyone went to sleep, I redid her hair the way she wore it. She groomed me to be a hairdresser and didn't even know it, neither did I.

After she died, my mother also did hair, and I was yet being groomed. I began to practice pressing and curling her hair. Birthed out of this training was a desire to become a cosmetologist. Even though I didn't pursue cosmetology as a trade right after high school, I did hair right in my kitchen from 1977-1980. After TRW abruptly closed in September 1980, I went straight to Lenoir Community College (LCC-Kinston, N.C.) and enrolled. I got my cosmetology license while I was studying for a business degree. After receiving my Associates Degree in business, I received my cosmetology instructor's license, and became a Cosmetology instructor.

God enabled me to reach these goals within 2 years. I worked at Grocery Fair as a cashier to help pay my way through college. The grooming continued. After teaching for two years at LCC, I started doing hair at North Queen Beauty Salon, where the founder and owner is Patricia Dunn Best. I named the station I worked at "Edna's Corner." I worked there for eight years. My tenure there was amazing. This was the first crew that I worked with for the eight years I was there.

North Queen Beauty Salon, Queen Street, Kinston, N.C. Founder & Owner: Patricia A. Best

From left top: Patricia A. Best, Kathy McNair, Edna Hall, Linwood Williams, Cynthia B. Bryant, Sheryl D. Cooper, and Faye Gooding. Others not pictured that joined us later are James Dixon, Mary Brown, Ann Davis, and Gwen Langston.

I worked with the sweetest ladies ever and two gentlemen from 1984-1992. At the time, I worked at North Queen, my sister, Geraldine Speight-now deceased, was also being groomed. She went to LCC in Kinston, N.C. and became a cosmetologist, as well. She came in the shop one day after class and told.

Patricia that one day she was going to take me away from her. After being groomed in how to run a business, she made good of her promise. In February 1992, S & H Creative Hair Designs was established in Snow Hill, N.C. The S stood for Speight and the H stood for Hall. We became business partners from February 1992 until April 2000. Going to work was exciting. There was never a dull moment. Our business strived.

During our time of partnership, other cosmetologists were groomed through our business. They were already bootlegging in their homes but decided to join us. They were such profound hairstylists: Marian Jones, Becky Best Walker, Angela Joyner Meyers, Addie Hooker, Evelyn Campbell, Tameka Grant, Darrick Shackleford, Jean

Speight, Veronica Yelverton and Sheila Johnson. We were all great stylists. All ten of us had our own unique styling techniques.

When Geraldine came out of remission, it was difficult. Some days, I had to give her shots, but it was ok because I loved her so much. Geraldine had leukemia, but she never let that hold her back from doing whatever she wanted to do. In 1997, we relocated to Kinston, N.C. One day she got a call from her doctor saying she needed to come to their office right then. On that day our lives changed forever. She went to Winston Salem and went through chemotherapy and radiation, but she was strong. She passed away April 2, 2000, at the age of 37.

I was devastated. She and I had done everything together. It was so hard going to work and not seeing her. I kept the name S and H until 2007. When we moved the business to Kinston, N.C., we downsized from 7 to 4 booths. I stayed on 258 North for 10 years. I changed the name to Edna's Corner after I moved the shop to my home on Poole Road. My husband became ill, and it was easier to take care of him being at the house. No matter where I relocated, my customers followed me, and I thank them from the bottom of my heart. They remained loyal until I had to close the salon down in March 2020, due to the Corona virus pandemic. I'm still a cosmetologist and serve funeral homes when called upon, especially Albritton Carraway Funeral Home. I've been working with them since 1980. I serve as a grief counselor and hairstylist when needed.

Life can have lots of twists and turns as you travel from birth to adulthood. It is all a part of the grooming process. There will be bad days, good days, hard days, difficult days, easy days, mind boggling days, and down outright mind-blowing days, but it is all a part of the process. All your days won't be bad days. All your days won't be good days. You will fall and you will get up. Paul said he was the chief of sinners. I too have come short of the glory of God.

Galatians 5:19-21 (KJV) says, "19 Now the works of the flesh are manifest, which are these; Adultery, fornication, uncleanness, lasciviousness, 20 Idolatry, witchcraft, hatred, variance, emulations, wrath, strife, seditions, heresies, 21 Envyings, murders, drunkenness, revellings, and such like: of the which I tell you before, as I have also told you in time past, that they which do such things shall not inherit the kingdom of God." I've entertained some of these spirits. Mercy pled my case. I confessed them, repented of them, and turned from them. God forgave me and I'm grateful.

One thing I've learned these 60+ years of life is that my good days have far outweighed my bad days. The grooming has been bittersweet, but I made it! In the words of Marvin Sapp's "I Thank Him for It All," he says, God, "I thank You for it all: the good, bad, the ugly, great, and small, the times of victory, and when I fall. I'm so grateful that I'm still standing tall. I thank You for my tears. The pain helped me overcome my fears. You've been good to me down throughout the years. It's a miracle that I'm still standing here. All that I am is because of all that You brought me through. And everything I survived, it's all because of You." The lyrics continue:

"How can I say thank You for all the ways you made for me (I can't thank You enough) The doors You opened.

The times you were there always making a way for me (I can't thank You enough)

I cannot express the gratitude that I feel for You right now (I can't thank You enough)

So, I just have to pause for a moment right now and say. I gotta say thank You,

For all You've done for me

Oh, thank You, for every opportunity.

I gotta say thank You, I gotta tell You thank You, for all the ways You made.

I just wanna say, "Thank You, for my life···for my health, Thank You."

I say yes, even when it was bad.

On this road, Arba Road, now called Hull Road, in a little spot called Arba I was propelled into my destiny. I could either grow through it or die in it. Eventually, I chose to grow through it. Growing pains are horrible at times, especially when it doesn't line up with what you have in mind. I wasn't always a willing vessel. There were times my disobedience landed me in some bad situations. The consequences almost cost me my life. On this road, my destiny could have been cut short. God led me from tragedy to triumph. I could have gone to prison for murder twice on this road. Yes, life for me was no crystal stair, but God kept me through it all. I learned some hard lessons that I glean from today. I had a choice to let life as I knew it destroy me or take charge of my life by surrendering to the will of God in my life. I chose to give it all to Jesus and live. Through God, I triumphed over my enemy.

CHAPTER FOUR

FROM TRAGEDY TO TRIUMPH

Psalm 41:9-13 KJV -"9 Yea, mine own familiar friend, in whom I trusted, which did eat of my bread, hath lifted up his heel against me. 10 But thou, O Lord, be merciful unto me, and raise me up, that I may requite them. 11 By this I know that thou favourest me, because mine enemy doth not triumph over me. 12 And as for me, thou upholdest me in mine integrity, and settest me before thy face forever. 13 Blessed be the Lord God of Israel from everlasting, and to everlasting. Amen, and Amen."

Losing my grandmother was one of the worst days of my life. I was only 12 years old. Losing her left me lonely, angry, frustrated, and numb. I didn't understand why she left me. It was almost like my breath was snatched right out of me. Even now, 54 years later, it brings tears to my eyes. I really miss her a lot. She made sure I was in church every 2nd and 4th Sunday. Prayer meetings and convocations were my life. Her friend, Sarah Newbern, made sure I stayed in church after she passed away. I sang in the youth choir at St. John United Holiness Church

(U.H.C.). Only the picture of the spot it once sat in is pictured below. I loved going to church and it was a part of the process. St. John U.H.C. is where I began to be groomed for ministry under Reverend Rufus McAllister. The pastor now is Apostle Michael Artis.

Where the Old Church the New St. John Holiness Church and St. John Kingdom Ministries. This is where I received Christ as my personal savior at the age of 11. I remained a member there until

April 1972. Being a Christian so young was difficult because it wasn't the norm for young children to be saved. After my grandmother and Mrs. Sarah died, I studied with the Jehovah Witnesses until I got my driver's license. I went back to my church and began to work faithfully. I also attended Brown's Chapel F.W.B. Church in Snow Hill, N.C. in the Brown town community because it was in walking distance. It was there that I met Pastor/Bishop E. O. Edwards, now deceased.

My father in the gospel was so calm and easy, but firm. He taught me how to be a good follower and a good leader. He groomed me in ministry. He always said, "Edna, the word is line upon line and precept upon precept, so stay with the word and you will be alright." After I preached my initial sermon in October of 1977, he put me right to work. Under his tutoring, I learned how to stand tall in the midst of adversity.

In life we all sin and come short of the glory of God. We venture out trying to be like our peers because we don't fit in as a Christian. This causes us to go through stuff that may or may not have been a part of the plan that God had mapped out for us. Even though He can take your mistakes and grow you through them, it would have been a lot different had we just followed His plan. The roads we choose in life can take us to some terrible, dark, unchartered places. Grooming can be as easy as we allow it or as hard as we make it. It's easy when we yield to the Holy Spirit and not rebel against it. When we choose our way, it leads to destruction.

Proverbs 14:12 KJV - "There is a way which seemeth right unto a man, but the end thereof are the ways of death."

Groomed to survive. This is Arba Road, Snow Hill, N.C.—now known as Hull Road. I lived on this road for most of my life with my grandmother "Dodge" until she died in November 1967. This was a road of life and death. I was groomed for life. I tried to take someone else's life and tried to take my own life on this road. I laid in a field, hiding from my attempted rapist on this road. God has always been with me, shielding me from hurt harm and danger. I never would have made it without Him. Therefore, if you wonder why I am so head strong about Jesus, this is why.

When you don't know a person's story, don't judge their praise. God has kept me from jail and hell, and I thank Him for it all. I am not including the names of the people because my aim is not to hurt anyone. I have forgiven them and have been forgiven for my disobedience. I'm healed and delivered. The experience has enabled me to help others who have gone through sexual abuse and groom them to help others.

On October 24, 1970, I went out to a club located in Hookerton, N.C. called Little Paradise, trying to hang like my friends. When my date skipped out on me, I chose to still try and party. From the womb, I was ordained to be a warrior for Christ. Instead of going home because it was so early, I decided to hang out a little longer. Trying to hang can get you hung. The word says in 1st Corinthians 10:12-13 (KJV) "12 Wherefore let him that thinketh he standeth take heed lest he fall. 13 There hath no temptation taken you but such as is common to man: but God is faithful, who will not suffer you to be tempted above that ye are able; but will with the temptation also make a way to escape, that ye may be able to bear it."

God knew that I was heading for trouble. When God showed me the escape route, I ignored Him. I didn't take it. The road I took almost cost me my life. This road, Highway 58 North, leading from Highway 13 in Snow Hill, N.C . to Wilson, N.C. will forever be labeled in my heart as, "The Road of Terror." There's a place called Cherry's Inn on this road that signifies where my nightmare began. The driver, whose name I never knew, decided he was going to rape me. All the way down that road he kept saying to me, "Oh, you going to be one of those that play hard to get, hey?" Those words are forever engraved in my head. I was literally sitting on the doorknob, terrified and lost.   He kept saying he had to go to his grandmother's house. Even though I did not take the first door of escape, God had another one on reserve.

After turning down a dirt path right beside Cherry's Inn, he attacked me. I fought for my dear life. I escaped and ran toward the highway, only to be caught, but this time God had intervened. God blocked it. He wouldn't let it be. After he couldn't get pass my guardian angel, he became angry and frustrated. He said, "I'm not taking you home, but I'll leave you here in Stantonsburg, and you can find you a way home." Even though I was born in Stantonsburg, I don't remember ever going back there. I had no clue where I was.

As long as I was away from him I didn't even care. He left me at another club in Stantonsburg. I went in crying and distraught only to find I had some cousins there. Immediately they went into action trying to catch the guy but to no avail. I was offered a ride home. This same night, on this same road, Highway 58, The Road of Terror, led to more terror. Instead of being taken home, the driver turned down a dirt path that led to a church, a church where I had praised God, sang in the choir, and ushered. The two men decided they would do a train rape on me. Again, God blocked it.

My guardian angel was still working on my behalf, even though I was disobedient the earlier part of the night; he never left me. They couldn't beat my guardian angel. The other guy told him to stop. I had freaked out. There's a thin line between sane and insane. I found a screwdriver in the foot of the car and was prepared to stab him to death if he got in that back seat. He was so mad, he backed up out of the woods extremely fast. He did it so fast and so hard until it knocked some bricks out of place on the church.

He put me and the other guy out on Highway 58, The Road of Terror. By now, my brain is in disarray. We were soon picked up by my cousins that were at the club earlier. I stayed with some relatives the rest of the night. Before day, I could feel hands fondling me. Born Thursday, December 23, 1954, in Stantonsburg, N.C. was a miracle. October 24, 1970, in this same town, I began to think about ending my life. I wanted to end it all. I said, if this is how I'm going to have to live the rest of my life, I'd rather be dead. By daylight I was done. Killing myself was the only way out of this nightmare.

My mind was made up. On Sunday, Oct. 25, 1970, around 8 a.m., I put the plan in motion. After being the victim of an attempted rape twice in one night, in less than an hour apart, I decided I didn't want to live anymore. Yes, I am well, aware of that suicidal demon—again, being groomed for my destiny. I began to walk towards Arba Road with both of my eyes closed. I was walking middle way of the road, hoping somebody would run over me and kill me. Again, God blocked it. He had great plans for me. I just didn't know it at that time, and I didn't even care. I agree with Rich Tolbert, Jr. when he wrote, "God knows the plans He has for me. He knows the thoughts He thinks toward me, and nothing is an accident. I'm alive because there's more."

I later found out that Satan was not done. He was determined to take me out. His threefold mission is to steal, kill and to destroy. He doesn't care what he must do to accomplish that goal. One night after attending a basketball game at Greene Central High School with whom I thought was a friend, I encountered another attempt of gang rape. I took the Bible serious. Having sex before marriage is a sin. They took the other girl home first and cut through the woods, saying it was a shortcut to my house. Instead, they had plotted earlier that night to rape me. As I said earlier, the same road, "Arba Road", where I had earlier tried to take my life, was the road I escaped to after laying in a field for over an hour.

In the woods, the guy I went to the game with claimed he had to use the bathroom. It was all a part of their plot to rape me. When the driver tried to climb in the backseat with me, I began to kick and fight. Suddenly, I could see the other guy come around to the other side of the car to help him. God gave me supernatural strength to break free and get out of the car and run. I didn't know where, but I just kept running until I began to hear dogs barking. I'm afraid of dogs, but at that point I chose to be eaten alive by dogs than to be raped.

I ran pass the house, which was the house where my date lived, into the field. The field was right in front of the house. I just laid there, terrified. I could hear them calling my name, but I wouldn't move. I was so scared to get up and scared to keep laying there, and scared I would be bitten by a snake. I was wishing I could just die and never be found. But, again, God blocked it. He wouldn't let it be. He had a plan for me.

Then I could hear the guy I went to the game with telling me to come out and he would take me home. He kept shining the light in the field, so I decided to take a chance and come out. He took me home, which was right up the road. I drove a school bus during that time, and I told him if he tried to get on my bus, that I would run over him and kill him dead.

Disobedience can land you in some hard places. When you have been misused, your mind can travel to some places you may not ever go. He didn't believe me, so the next morning, when he stepped his foot on that road, I put my bus in gear to run over him. God is a keeper of the mind. I am so thankful that He was always there for me, even when I would turn a deaf ear to His instructions. Being groomed can sometimes be painful. Those traumatic episodes helped to make me who I am today. I am very sensitive to people that have been traumatized sexually, mentally, physically, and emotionally. Amid all of this, I stayed focused. On April 17, 1971, I met a young man named Isaac Hall. I graduated from high school on June 3, 1973 and started working afterwards. Isaac and I got married on November 9, 1973. The grooming continued from graduation to marriage, and six years later into childbearing.

Graduation: 6/3/1973

Hull Road F.W.B. Church (Kinston, N.C.)

Groomed in ministry: These two churches ironically played a vital part in my life. Each of them taught me cleanliness—cleansing of the temple: the physical temple we go to worship in on Sundays and our temple wherein the Holy Spirit resides. Our bodies are God's temple.

1st Corinthians 6:19 (KJV)

"What? know ye not that your body is the temple of the Holy Ghost which is in you, which ye have of God, and ye are not your own?"

The building we worship in is called a temple.

1st Kings 6:17 (KJV)

"And the house, that is, the temple before it, was forty cubits long."

We are instructed to keep both clean. Jesus said He will not dwell in an unclean temple. The word also says in 1st Corinthians 3:17 (KJV), "If any man defile the temple of God, him shall God destroy; for the temple of God is holy, which temple ye are."

As a child, my grandmother would clean the first church that was located on Arba Road. I learned how to clean the church from top to bottom, always checking behind myself to make sure I hadn't missed any spots. The second one, located in Kinston, N.C., is where I learned how to work out my salvation with fear and trembling. I learned how to possess my own vessel with fear and trembling. I learned how to bring my flesh under subjection. I learned how to live a sanctified and holy life. Am I perfect? No. Do I mess up sometimes? Yes. When I do fall short, I quickly repent. I learned how to do teamwork. Under the leadership of Bishop Ernest Edwards and Apostle Rudolph Williams, I learned how to endure hardness as a good soldier.

I served a total of 28 years at Hull Road. I served 14 years under each pastor. Elder Romas Dixon was my first District Union #1 president. In this picture, other than our leaders, you will see our team. Each of us has different callings and spiritual giftings, but we worked together as a team to further the gospel of Jesus Christ.

Proverbs 27:17 (KJV)

"Iron sharpeneth iron; So a man sharpeneth the countenance of his friend."

This we did and still do watch out for each other and support each other whenever we can. Pictured is Evangelist Ruth Morris Edwards, Dr. Edna Hall, Pastor Dalphine Hart, Pastor James Powell, Pastor Walter Cannon, and Dr. Andre' Cannon. Others that joined the team later are Pastor Barbara Sutton, Eldress Delores Cotton, Eldress Gwendolyn Gaylor, and Eldress Lucy Koonce. We were groomed well. We love each other dearly.

Initial Sermon: 10/03/1977 - Hull Road

Honorary Doctorate in Psychology and
Christian Counseling & Doctorate in Psychology
and Theological Studies

CHAPTER 5

FROM TRIUMPH TO TRAILBLAZER

2 Corinthians 2:14 KJV -"Now thanks be unto God, which always causeth us to triumph in Christ, and maketh manifest the savour of his knowledge by us in every place."

We often wonder as children where we will end up in our adult life. We make plans but sometimes they don't work out like we planned. I have learned that there is a plan that is greater than ours, whose designer is God. He says in Jeremiah 29:11, "For I know the thoughts that I think toward you, saith the Lord, thoughts of peace, and not of evil, to give you an expected end." I am so glad that after all God has brought me through, I still have joy. I understand in full what this scripture means. I lived it.

Peter 1:3-5, 7-8 KJV -"···according as his divine power hath given unto us all things that pertain unto life and godliness, through the knowledge of him that hath called us to glory and virtue: whereby are given unto us exceeding great and precious promises: that by these ye might be partakers of the divine nature, having escaped the corruption that is in the world through lust. And beside this, giving all diligence, add to your faith virtue; and to virtue knowledge; and to godliness brotherly kindness; and to brotherly kindness charity. For if these things be in you, and abound, they make you that ye shall neither be barren nor unfruitful in the knowledge of our Lord Jesus Christ."

I admonish you to not neglect the gift that is within you. Be the vessel of good use for the Kingdom of God that He has created you to be. The words of Paul in 2nd Corinthians 4:15-18 KJV says, "For all things are for your sakes, that the abundant grace might through the thanksgiving of many redound to the glory of God. For which cause we faint not; but though our outward man perish, yet the inward man is renewed day by day. For our light affliction, which is but for a moment, worketh for us a far more exceeding and eternal weight of glory; while we look not at the things which are seen, but at the things which are not seen: for the things which are seen are temporal; but the things which are not seen are eternal."

ABOUT THIS BOOK

This book will help you to accept what God allowed and is allowing in your life, whether it is good or bad. It will help you to take an inventory of your life and show you where it could have been worse. This book will show you how God created you to be a helper to someone else who is suffering the same things you have been through. It will induce a deeper sense of the gift of discernment that has been given to you. Things you once took for granted, you will see that it was for your good and not your bad. It will heighten your sensitivity and make you aware of others who are trapped inside of their past and pain.

DR. EDNA RUTH HOOKER HALL

ABOUT THE AUTHOR

I was born December 23, 1954, in Stantonsburg, N.C., to the late Hattie Bell Hooker and the late Raymond Wooten. I was raised and groomed by my grandmother, Alice Edwards, until she passed away in 1967. I have 17 other siblings, 4 have passed away. I graduated from Greene Central High School, Snow Hill, N.C., in 1973. I was married 44 years to the late Isaac Hall. I have three children. I am the Pastor/Founder of Chara Ministries Deliverance Center & Chara's Community & Developmental

Complex, Inc. I serve as the administrative assistant to the Bishop of Northwest B Conference of The United American FWB Denomination. I serve also as the registrar of the United American FWB Denomination to The National Convention of FWB Churches, Inc. I am a member of NWB District 1 and serve as the choir director.

* 9 7 9 8 8 8 9 5 5 5 2 2 3 *